MW01245898

Broken Addict, Fractured Recovery

Bernard Zeitler

Copyright © 2022 Bernard Zeitler

All rights reserved.

ISBN: 9798410807920

DEDICATION

In writing this book I struggled with things and found a mindfulness that brings hope. This book is dedicated to those who feel hopeless, discouraged and hurt. It is dedicated to those who found recovery and maybe didn't realize that addiction is a chronic condition. It is dedicated to all who came before and who will come after me. May it provide hope and insight to anyone willing to read it with an open mind.

CONTENTS

ACKNOWLEDGMENTS

I want to thank everyone from around the world who has encouraged me and especially those who discouraged me with their challenges. I also want to thank God as I understand Him to be for giving me a vision of recovery that helped me realize something more important than what some pushed upon me.

Finally thank you to some special people who gave me courage to step forth on this journey.

My wife, Susan, without whom I may never have started writing. Her patience and sometimes frustration at my inattentiveness when the words and thoughts were flowing fast from the mind to paper.

Some people who know who they are from Tasmania, Canada, many different states in the US and places like Malta, Wales, Ireland, Scotland, England, Kenya and so many more places. Thank you Poppy, John, Jennifer, Lori, Tracy and so many more.

An extra special thank you also goes to Remedy Max, MA, BA, DRI-ABCP for authoring a special chapter at the end of this book and for being an editorial advisor.

An Overview:

The question of how to define addiction has been going on since the beginning of time. Some have said it is a choice. Others an 'allergy'. Still others view it as a disease. Considering that addiction is in many ways all of these and none of these. This book argues that it is a disease of choice's broken, allergies flaring up and a disease of the deepest nature.

Broken addict looks at the progress from a Choice or an Allergy to a disease.

1. How the disease process of addiction progressively gets worse.

2. What is the difference between the disease as a family and the forms it takes?

3. Is it possible to begin treating one family member of the disease and miss another one?

In looking at the second part as Fractured Recovery, we look at key points of treatment considering the possibility that what is missing has more to do with change than with a focus on the single form.

1. Why is relapse common?

2. Does a person potentially have a relapse that involves a different form?

3. Can recovery be hindered by hidden relapses? (Relapses that look like recovery on the surface).

Beginning with some overview from a personal note of the author we will go into the questions from the angle of a hope of recovery rather than the limitations of the individual disease family members. After each chapter there will be a section to write down thoughts.

STARTING THE JOURNEY

To start this journey it might help to introduce myself and share my background in broad terms.

My name is Bernard and I am an addict in recovery. I don't think I was always an addict but life throws things at you and it changes you. For me that began with being born premature and the youngest of 4 children. Maybe I was destined to be addicted because of that rough start but we may never know.

Before I started school I watched as my older brother died in front of me. In the late 60's we lived on a main highway and Jon (my older brother) was hit by a car, killing him instantly.

Over the first 20 years of my life I also lost one of my 2 sisters, several cousins, and an uncle. But the losses are part of living and so it continues.

My educational background after graduating from high school started with studying to be a minister teaching, Psychology which led to Social work (which I finally completed in 1991) and other careers.

My path to recovery led me through addictions I only now recognize and finally to recovery from Compulsive Gambling. So what were the other addictions?

All of them were, as I look back, a wagering of my life based on chance or my own skill. Over the last 5 decades I have been a smoker, food addict, pop addict, thrill seeker, emotional mess and so much more. Most of these were intermixed with some form of gambling in more conventional ways.

On November 21, 2007, after months of searching for something to help me regain my footing, I walked into my second GA meeting and began recovery. The week before I had attended and while I knew that I had an addiction, I didn't think it was 'that bad'. After that first meeting I went a block away, bought a $1 scratch off ticket and in that moment I knew that I had a problem. I had just taken the 20 question 'test', passing with flying colors (even with my attempts to lie so I wouldn't). I also had just finished listening to stories of how people had lost jobs, went to prison and pretty much every possible pain was put forth because of their gambling. How could I leave a meeting and spend even a penny on such things?

Leading up to this 'epiphany' of sorts I had had my own trail of pain which started on Wednesday, January 17, 2007 with the death of my mother. After she died, I started searching for help because in the 16 days leading up to her death I was not as focused on her needs as I should have been. The day she came home from the hospital for hospice I took a 'shortcut' to get home which took me twice as long, all so I could stop and buy some scratch off tickets on the way there. Just as I realized how messed up my gambling after a meeting was, I saw the messed up thinking of taking a shortcut that was unfamiliar to me.

On my journey to November 21, 2007 I tried counseling, different kinds of meetings and even considered suicide. The lead up to the first meeting involved nearly losing 1 of my jobs and becoming so depressed that I spent time on a mental health unit for suicidal depression.

Even after the beginning of meetings I struggled with depression to the point of suicide but found a path forward. The next four years were spent 'working' the program and following the example of others. People would tell me how the program worked and encourage me to work it in the same way. I even worked with people and expected they would have the same results. Alas that was not what I experienced.

On December 26, 2010 things again had a shift. My dad died shortly after midnight (keeping a promise he made not to die on Christmas day). This experience was different though as I had a chance to make things right with my dad before he died. The 'amends' was not a spoken one or one that people might recognize as such. On the cover of the book and below is the way I made amends. I had begun doing bike repair and assembly for one of my jobs and that was something that tied into my dad's love of fixing and building things. By the time we worked on the bike together he was not as capable of the fine motor skills required to repair bikes but he could paint them. As amends we worked together with little talk of the past and focused on the task at hand. We restored a bike that had sat in a barn exposed to the harsh Michigan weather for about 25 or so years. We were not able to repair the headlight but that old Sears bike was almost like new when we were done.

Fast forward a little while and my journey put me through a divorce of my choosing and an event that changed my perspective on recovery forever. Just before the divorce was final I ended up in the hospital diagnosed with Asthma. The events that led to a fateful encounter with another addict who saw my anxiousness and knew I was feigning for a meeting. Without knowing what my addiction was I was approached and asked about it.

In the conversation I was asked about what meeting I was missing. The conversation went from the idea of the addiction to something that seemed familiar but somewhat foreign too. Both of us were working on getting better from different addictions but the path was the same! This was where the vision and focus of People Growing Hope & Recovery was given life.

I realized that recovery was the treatment for the disease in a different way. The 'program' was for the disease and started with targeted treatment. Like many diseases that have several forms, the treatment is the same with it starting where the disease presents. Cancer is a disease that comes in many different forms but all are treated with the same treatment adjusted for the specific form and then targeted at constant checkups. The checkups are not just for the form that was treated initially but also for the forms that are potential recurrences.

Now comes the purpose of this book:

"Broken Addict Fractured Recovery" is a walk through addiction as a disease that destroys everything in its path. That starts with the addict themselves. In telling about the different events that led to me seeking recovery, a picture of shattered hope and purpose is seen. Recovery began as a focused process with fine-tuned precision on the form of my visible addiction. But in time that fine-tuned precision became limited and ineffective because it only looked at the past and a single part of life. Much like the headlight in the bike, it looked good but didn't really have much purpose in the big picture. My recovery was 'Fractured" while it was not completely destroyed, it was not really functional. I needed to go further.

What happens when you fix a shattered pot but don't take into account the whole pot as a vessel? Doesn't it look good until you pour the water in it and the water is not contained?

Thus it is with recovery that an addict is broken into a million pieces (shattered) when the process begins. The focus is on simply getting the addiction to a place where it 'looks good' and not going beyond that to being functional in a larger sense.

Recovery begins with the broken (shattered) and getting it to a point of fracture (functional appearance). To go further takes a lifetime. The healing begins when the work moves into a fuller restoration.

This book looks at the broken addict as a starting point and realizing that to heal an addict one must first find a point of fracture (bringing the addiction into a functional state).

And so we begin a journey. Hopefully the words that follow are ones that make sense, resonate with the reader and offer a shared perspective. The book before this one talked of history and how People Growing Hope & Recovery began. Now it is time to get a bit more personal and look at the steps of a program which is defined in many different ways. We recognize the reality that recovery is not a 'one size fits all' process. Recovery is dynamic and should be embraced as such.

ACTIVITY SECTION
(Offers designated activity pages between chapters)

What Hit Home for You?

Consider what has been read and take time to 'digest' it. Then use this designated page to write down your thoughts

THE SHATTERED ADDICT

When addiction starts it is a mystery that can only be answered with the realization that it is not about when it is first noticed. With any disease there is a time when it seems to be just a 'normal' part of life. It is not until the symptoms are visible that help is sought.

When we get a virus it may not be noticed at first because it has a "gestation period" or time that it begins to interact with a person without visible symptoms. The same happens with many diseases. Addiction is no different. Consider the Covid virus or even Cancer. When does a person get it and when do they bring themselves to seek treatment?

The disease has to grow a bit before it becomes noticeable. So in reality it is present well before it is treated. Sometimes the symptoms of a cold are so mild that it seems 'manageable' or can be mistaken for an 'allergy' which we assume will pass. But over time the disease or infection just festers more and becomes worse. On occasion what was thought to be a cold or simply something that would be mild requires more attention. Why is that? Is it because what was thought to be one thing was really something else?

A personal example from life that might help demonstrate this is when I was sick and thought it was a cold then as it got worse I assumed it was Bronchitis (Something that I got chronically). What happened is that a point came when I decided I needed to get help so I went to the Emergency Room and was given medications.

I called back a little later with a question and was asked to return to the hospital. They even offered an ambulance to come get me. Why? Because a test came back indicating something very serious was making me ill.

Once I drove back, the test results were revealed to me and I was admitted to the hospital. What was really different is that the test was not correct and neither was I. I ended up having asthma (which I deal with to this day).

All indications are that I have had asthma for most of my life but only when it became so severe was it made possible for it to be discovered.

As an addict I would suggest that it was not something that started out as a full blown addiction that was clear and visible to anyone. It may even have been around for a long time and thought to be something else. It wasn't until I experienced a symptom so severely that led me to seek treatment. In seeking treatment the condition had crafted all the little cracks designed to shatter me into many pieces with respect to living.

So I was a shattered person. Everything that was being held together for years was no longer held together. Now what?

I had to focus on the Asthma first as that is the disease at hand but life keeps bringing in new issues. So once the Asthma was dealt with other things were able to be addressed.

As an addict I first address the primary disease form and as time progresses I start dealing with new diseases either related to the original or something new. That is the point of going from targeted treatment to a maintenance and monitoring process. Knowing that my gambling is treated, I now focus on what could replace it.

A shattered addict may not find recovery but that is when the treatment is most likely to be started.

The steps involve getting the target addressed in the initial treatment. That said recovery is not guaranteed when the shattered addict begins the process.

Consider what it means to be a shattered addict. Is it simply focused on the addiction that is seen or the hidden aspects? Things like avoiding problems, past trauma and present life.

Common things looking back might be a traumatic loss, an undesirable childhood or any number of things that set the disease in motion. For me there were many shattering events that set in motion the search for relief. Now it is time to get into the discussion. Enough of how I believe things progressed to shatter life with addiction.

ACTIVITY SECTION

What Hit Home?

Consider what has been read and take time to 'digest' it. Then use this designated page to write down your thoughts.

GETTING STARTED

How do we define Addiction? Is it a choice? Is it an Allergy? Maybe it is a disease? Even today this argument is had in conversations. So what if it was all of these things and more?

How does an addiction start?

In reality we may never know the answer to this fully. But for some it involves peer pressure. Others have a health issue and are given medicine to relieve pain or address the issue for a time. Still others simply do something that seems fun or enjoyable at first.

Considering that addiction is in many ways all of these and none of these this book argues that it is a disease of choice's broken, allergies flaring up and a disease of the deepest nature. In this chapter let's look at each one to see the similarities and even a few of the anomalies that don't seem to fit.

Is it a Choice?

A choice first requires that there is more than one thing involved. In this sense addiction begins as a choice because there is a decision either to engage in the addiction or not to engage in it.

Does that mean we stop here though? Since the addiction begins with a single decision, some would say yes. If it is a decision it is always a decision. So this is where it begins, with a single decision but it still does not stop there.

A single decision can be a starting point for many things but it doesn't necessarily continue as a decision. Is there any disease that starts with a decision being made? If so then the decision may get things started but that is all it does.

Some diseases that are affected or can be caused by poor decisions or callous lifestyle choices can manifest as:

1. Heart Attacks.
2. Sugar Diabetes
3. Asthma.
4. Cancer
5. Hemorrhoids
6. Migraine Headaches
7. Kidney stones
8. Liver disease
9. Kidney disease
10. Arthritis
11. Common Cold
12. Viruses
13. Obesity
14. Carpal Tunnel
15. Broken Bones
16. Cuts, Bruises, Rashes etc.
17. Anxiety
18. Depression
19. Acne
20. Hemorrhoids

As you can see the single decision made is often a starting point for a disease. Granted many may not agree but it is a choice as to how a person looks at disease.

Is it an Allergy?

Well as we see above an Allergy, while having genetic and environmental aspects to it, also involves a choice. Once a person knows of an Allergy they can chose to avoid it, if possible, or learn how to manage and live with it. An example of an Allergy that cannot be avoided easily is 'House Dust". As a child I was told that I was allergic to house dust but because no amount of cleaning could possibly remove all house dust, I had to live with it. That said there are many things that can be done to lower the allergic reaction.

Maybe it is a disease?

Well now we are at the point of clarity. Since many, if not all diseases, have components of choice it makes sense that it is a progressive condition. While disease may have choice and may have components of an Allergic reaction, they also have other factors including genetics, culture, environment and even simple chance encounters.

An exercise in the process

Some interesting things to consider are examples of diseases that have a starting point of choice leading to the allergy and finally to the disease presenting.

Consider the examples below and ask yourself if it follows a pattern.

The Broken Leg Analogy

1. I chose where to walk or an activity (let's use getting on a swing and then jumping off it)

2. I find myself getting nervous and decide to get off the swing. (Maybe I jump from it)

3. I go a distance in the air until I land on the ground.

4. I landed in an unusual way and the result: a broken leg

At several points a choice was made followed by taking action.

A fear of heights or maybe distrust in the equipment results in a new choice.

I have an 'allergy' to a situation presenting in the symptom of fear or anxiety.

In trying to avoid the 'allergy' I take an action that ultimately results in a broken leg.

The Common Cold Analogy

1. I chose to go out into an environment where a foreign object (the virus) is floating around invisibly.

2. The foreign object (the virus) has contact with me and creates an 'allergic' reaction.

3. Time passes without awareness of this "allergic" reaction but as it worsens I experience the cold.

One choice (neither good nor bad) leads to exposure to a virus which affects me negatively.

I have a progressively worse 'allergic' reaction.

The 'allergic' reaction presents as a cold which, while usually not deadly, can be deadly if I do not attend to it earlier than later, as well as treating it in specific ways.

The process reviewed

While simple in the laying out of the 2 examples, few would disagree that each started with a choice (either conscious or unconscious) leading to an 'allergy' (or fear) real or imagined. Ultimately having an outcome that requires active treatment for the consequences (the disease).

With this underlying perspective we can start a journey of exploring addiction as a disease that is holistic in nature (one of the whole person, taking into account mental and social factors). Subsequently the disease will require treatment that is holistically based.

The recovery process demonstrated in the 12 Step fellowships starts off presenting the addiction as a single aspect of the disease but by the 12th step the truth is revealed that is often misunderstood or simply overlooked.

In Step 12 there are two phrases that emphasize the holistic nature of Addiction Recovery. Those Phrases are:

1. "Having Practiced"

2. "In All Our Affairs"

So it is that what recovery is about. A continuum of 'practice', where we work the treatment process AND broaden the 'treatment' to our whole way of living ("In All Our Affairs").

With this as a foundation we move forward into the process of the addiction that leads to a broken ("shattered") addict. Then following up with a look at how treatment can lead to a broken recovery. When done, focus is shifted towards how it might be possible to form a more whole recovery.

ACTIVITY SECTION

What Hit Home?

Consider what has been read and take time to 'digest' it.Now use this designated page to write down your thoughts.

WHERE TO BEGIN?

Do we know when that first decision was made to start the path to addiction? Is it possible to know or do we simply realize when we first became aware of it?

The sad truth is that like most diseases the first exposure may have come in a way that was innocent and had no significance in our memory. Like a cold or other viruses we may have a general idea of when it was introduced into our being without knowing the specifics. Some might even argue if it is truly material or even relevant identifying when or how one became exposed to the agent that made them ill. Should the real task at hand not be to focus on ways to prevent the disease from getting worse and finding ways to help one become healthier?

As a child an event happened and the brain began looking for a way to submerge the memory. Few people can tell every detail of their life from birth to the moment they are in. It is in these experiences that seemed like nothing that the first exposure happened. It may not even have any resemblance to the addiction that becomes visible.

So beginning is less about the first exposure than is when it became visible to us or to someone else. Some addictions can be 'invisible' for years until a situation arises that leaves no doubt. An example of how it may have happened comes from an interaction on a TV show called "Monk" in the discussion he was having with his Psychiatrist he discovers something very unusual. The conversation went like this:

> A: There's something I never told you.
> Something happened when I was a boy
> There was an incident.
> With a...with a man.
>
> D: Who was that?
>
> A: I'd never seen him before. Stranger.
>
> D: How old were you?

A: I don't remember. Young.
I was... so small.
I remember...I remember I was naked.

D: Take your time.

A: I was so naked. I just hated being naked.
And I remember...I was crying.
And then...he hit me.

D: Adrian, I'm so sorry.

A: There was blood. There was blood everywhere.
I was screaming. I wanted him to stop.
And my mother...my mother was smiling.

D: W- w-wait, your-your mother was there?

A: Why didn't she stop him? She was supposed to protect me. He kept hitting me. Swinging me around upside down, and...

D: You were upside down? Was he wearing a mask?

A: I never wanted to be naked again.

D: Adrian, that man was a doctor. You're remembering your own birth.

A: Doctor... doctor?

D: Anybody else, I wouldn't have believed it. But you...

A: Doctor? Mm-hmm. Well, that would explain a lot, actually. The lights, and my father in the doorway holding a balloon.

D: You feel better?

A: Yes. I do. Wow. That only took 11 years.

This example is a bit exaggerated but for the purpose of figuring out where it began it makes a point. Many times the memory is suppressed or not necessarily as important as what we do to move forward in recovery. It also gives insight into something else.

At the end of the exchange with Monk it becomes clear that, for him it took "only 11 years" of therapy to get to that awareness. Interestingly enough he did not count from the time of the event that happened (about 50 years) but rather from the point that he began the process.

The idea is not about going back and rehashing it but rather working to move forward by becoming aware of it. Patience is key as many times the process starts with the desire to change rather than the desire to know the why. Over time we may piece together a part of the puzzle and it may help but again we may never get to that point. In that sense the real point is moving forward from what was growing as we move forward without necessarily digging up a past that is not going to change by being dug up. Besides, delving deep into the past takes consumes precious energy and time, both of which can better serve us in the present as we focus on our healing journey.

Where do we begin? We begin with the desire to change. In 12 Step programs the statement goes like this:

"The only requirement for membership is a desire to stop (drinking, gambling etc.)."

So start with the desire to change and stop the addiction. Remember something when considering this though. Often desire and urge are referenced together. They have the same meaning and in light of that it is likely that the desire/ urge to stop exists because there is also a desire/ urge to continue.

A desire to stop is tied to the previous desire to engage in the addiction. They are often both present together. For instance, when active in addiction a person desires to continue with little real regard for the pain.

Also while in active addiction, the pain brings the desire not to continue. How often has an addict had such a bad experience that they say "NEVER AGAIN?" or "I am not going to do that again." only to return to active addiction next time the urges hit?

In remembering that every desire or urge exists with an equal and opposite desire / urge the key becomes learning to create an environment that encourages the desire to stop / change as going forward has the strongest pull. The question of where to begin becomes clear if it is tied to the desire to stop.

So we begin with that moment of clarity when the desire to stop is present and strong enough that we take action or are given the directive by family, friends, a court or some other event compelling us to stop / change our self-destructive behavior.

Knowing that the desire to stop is there and it is not alone can be scary. Knowing this can also be empowering because it gives one new hope. The path forward now is what to do with the hope and how can it be used to make those necessary changes?

ACTIVITY SECTION

What Hit Home?

Consider what has been read and take time to 'digest' it. Now use this designated page to write down your thoughts.

TWO DESIRES

With the starting point of awareness comes the new process of what to do with it. How does recovery emerge from the awareness of two desires battling within me?

In life we experience this desire dichotomy in almost every aspect of our day. Handling them can be an automatic thing or a conscious decision but seldom is it handled alone. Emotions, People in our life and even our own belief system create the responses. Before going on let's look at some examples of desires (urges) that are competing. What does it look like to have "automatic" and conscious processes related to these desires?

Automatic Desires handled

What happens when a person breathes? Is there a desire there? Consider the person with 'sleep apnea' and what happens.

Our body has a need for oxygen and thus our brain processes the need knowing that the lungs help with the process. It sends out a signal telling our lungs to breathe (including every aspect of the process).

The brain handles every need of the body with signals to the different areas that handle the process.

Now consider the brain having a desire to take a break. It 'forgets' to send out the signals for breathing and everything stops for a bit.

The brain desired rest and thus a desire not to breathe for that moment. The lungs then send a signal to the brain (along with every other area that needs the oxygen) the brain suddenly realizes the need to breathe again (along with every cell of the body) and sends the breathing signal again.

When the breathing stops the body experiences symptoms of withdrawal and doesn't like the feeling. This results in the desire to breathe being more powerful than the desire not to. Try testing this out by holding your own breath now and after a point you simply stop holding your breath! Why?

Conscious Desires handled

Eating is a conscious and automatic desire. It can be altered by eating disorders, cultural input and so many outside influences but at its core it is a process controlled by two opposing desires. The first part of it is the desire to eat which is triggered by a feeling of hunger. The second is the desire not to eat which is triggered by any number of things. (Feeling full, anxiety, Upset and the list goes on). The brain processes all the input and either triggers eating or triggers not eating.

The "Programmed" Desires

Programmed desires are ones that are unique in that they are 'triggered' by both the subconscious and conscious. The biggest difference is that they are 'targeted' to specific things. Hunger does not define what to eat because it is a desire of necessary processes. The base desires are part of a hierarchy of needs for survival. Targeted desires are not necessarily needed they are usually tied to emotions and memories.

I remember eating a candy bar when I was little and it resulted in feelings that connected with the taste, texture and the environment around me. As such I found a pleasant experience connected with eating Chocolate. Even today when I'm feeling depressed my thoughts go to Chocolate and other 'comfort foods'. This 'programmed' desire tends to become overwhelming at times and instead of simply eating a little and stopping I might eat several times what is healthy or reasonable (even if I am not hungry). These types of desires may well become addictions.

Now comes the handling of 2 Desires with respect to addiction (the disease of chosen allergy). Addiction falls under the 3rd area described as "Programmed" Desires. In 12 Step programs new people hear that the only requirement to join the fellowship is 'a desire to stop (whatever addiction the fellowship is for).

Something is often forgotten though. In the previous chapter we became aware of that key component.

That component: A DESIRE TO STOP IS NOT ALONE!

That's right, we can't have a desire to stop something we don't also have a desire to do in the first place.

So the starting point is recognizing the two desires that are present. One tells us to engage in the addiction and the other (which exists but for a long time was drowned out) says don't do it.

When the addiction has brought a person to their knees the desire which has been kept silent for a time comes in and says "you don't have to do this". For many it presents in statements like "I'm never going to do that again" or (as gamblers I know including myself have said) "I will never gamble again!'. This strong cry of a desire to stop, however painfully it comes out, seems to be short lived without some forms of both action and inaction.

The question comes to mind what action can or needs to be taken? That is where 12 Step fellowships, detox centers and all sorts of treatments come in. These provide a starting point and may even give a long term solution if the person is open minded. It can also lead to transferring the desire to something new that can be equally or more destructive if not careful.

So we began with awareness of this desire and the desire to stop what we have been doing which is separate from knowing when we started to change.

Now we are aware of the desire and how it works within our thinking. It is time to process what is needed to find peace with what was so we can move into what can be with recovery. It is time to accept the shattered wreck that addiction has made. It is both our chosen path and the disease that have laid waste to life. Now it is time to make a choice to treat the disease and rebuild life from those shattered pieces. Just as a person who has surgery to fix a broken leg and then goes to Physical Therapy so the leg becomes stronger... So we need to take ownership of treatment.

What does treatment look like? How do we do this?

ACTIVITY SECTION

What Hit Home?

Consider what has been read and take time to 'digest' it. Now use this designated page to write down your thoughts.

RECOVERY PROGRAM

Treatment is where we are but what does it look like? Some might say it is the 12 Step program. Still others might say it is religion or personal will power. There are even those who say it is hopeless. Each has some merit including the hopelessness. But all are the same process with personal beliefs guiding how it is seen.

Let's look at each 'treatment' with consideration to how it might work or not work. Starting with the last one first.

It's Hopeless

This is the idea that once an addict always an addict. Oddly this ties into some of the other treatments because we identify as the disease.

If it is hopeless then why even bother to try? Once a person gets to this point a choice is provided to the addict. Either accept what is and do nothing leading to more turmoil and insurmountable losses that will more likely than not result in death or to take the challenge and prove hopelessness wrong.

It creates the first sign of change because this point is where treatment begins. If it doesn't then acceptance and even suicide becomes the paved path for the addict.

It's Religion

"Finding Religion" is also an option that has specific outcomes.

Religion is a code of conduct with specific beliefs and can become a mission to 'convert everyone'. Sometimes it is good but it can also be very much a way to claim to be better than others. This too bleeds into the others. The 12 Step program, if taken as the set formula for recovery, can become more about getting people to believe the same and use the same process without treating the disease of addiction.

It's The 12 Step Program

While the 12 Steps are very clear as a guide, they may become so stringent that there is no room for individual perspective. As time has passed this option has been set up with very strict points of reference. Specific people may be given special standing (intentionally or unintentionally) due to the 'clean time' or holding an official position (host, treasurer, trustee etc.). Many fellowships have become more than simply a community to learn and practice the process. Even to the extent that, while the 'program' is the same for everyone, it becomes about the addiction of choice (Drinking, taking drugs, eating, gambling and so forth).

Now let's look at the "Recovery Program" as the foundation upon which healing happens without looking back at the addiction as 'special' or unique with respect to the process of healing.

The Program: As Unity Of Purpose

While there are 12 written steps that have been developed, the program didn't start out that way. It started out as a simple concept. As time went on it became more defined but that simple concept remained at the core. Without the concept the program is just a process that has been passed down through time. It is at its core a program of unity. The origin of the program has several renditions that demonstrate this.

I Fall Down... We Get Back Up

At the core is the recognition that the disease is tied to the individual alone (disconnected from others) which results in the disease growing. This is followed by connecting with others which is the treatment of the disease (disconnection). So addiction has no connection with the world around us and the treatment is connecting with the world around us (in a healthy balanced way).

Connection – Correction – Direction

Addiction is: separation – deterioration – deviation
Recovery is: connection – correction – Direction

This is a core of recovery programs which recognize that the disease is one of opposites. Recovery is a process of changing every aspect of living. In working recovery we start with looking at the addiction (disease) and seeing the progression.

First, the disease causes a separation from healthy practices of life. Before addiction started life consisted of being involved in life. The addiction begins there by taking over the time involved in activities a person does as a normal part of each day. It does not always cut everything off immediately but rather it starts small.

As the disease progresses it becomes more active and takes more and more connections away. This creates the break form everyday life as the normal process. The more the disease grows the further life deteriorates and the addict deviates (changes course) from all that gives their life meaning.

It is in this awareness that treatment can begin if the person is willing to wanting to change and a desire to stop.

Treatment begins with treating the separation caused by the disease (Symptom 1). The treatment for separation is connection (steps 1-3).

What does connection look like as a treatment? It starts with a desire to work on change (going to a meeting or connecting with others in some healthy way). So creating Connection becomes the initial treatment where a person recognizes there is a problem that they cannot handle alone.

Because it cannot be handled alone it makes sense that treatment starts with finding the connection needed with people who also have the disease of addiction (beginning with specific form). This connection becomes a foundation because in it we see the truth of an old adage: "I can do nothing alone but we can do anything together"

Recovery connects the addict who has a desire to change that is gaining strength. It may have been asleep for years but in the moment of clarity it reasserts itself and recovery begins.

As the power of connection begins to take hold treatment becomes a bit more powerful in that now it expands to rebuilding broken connections. To rebuild them correction begins. Deterioration (Symptom 2) is treated by correction (steps 4-9).

Often this treatment is seen as taking action which is focused on painful reviews of the past. In many ways this treatment is like having surgery because we look at the past and make changes (course corrections). It may involve direct interaction with people who have been affected by the addict's deteriorating condition but also has to have visible changes that are personal.

This second level of treatment is one that can be a bit more about what is done than what is said. The treatment compares to the old adage: "actions speak louder than words".

Because humans are not perfect, recovery is not always going to be perfect either. Change takes a lifetime and mistakes are bound to be made along the way. Relapses are not inevitable but they are likely depending on how the treatment progresses with respect to the disease. As the treatment continues to progress the last part becomes key to sustaining the treatment. Deviation (symptom 3) is treated by direction (steps 10 -12).

With connection and correction now being established it is time to consider the maintenance key to the treatment process. What is the purpose of recovery and working the previous treatment if there is "no Hope" of a permanent cure for the disease? The seeking purpose of the treatment aspect is so key that without it the other treatments are only temporary and superficial fixes. Meaning the addict may not be actively feeding their addiction by learning to abstain but they have not healed on the inside.

The treatment of deviation involves seeking direction and this is done differently depending on the individual. It does however have a very specific way of being done as it involves focusing on communication skills with ourselves and the power greater than self that we started with.

The final part of treatment is considered prayer and meditation. It has also been referred to as taking quiet time to just be present. In doing this we find the process returns to the beginning where we sought something greater than self-will.

Examples of this final part of treatment include the following examples:

1. A person I know in recovery practices both reaching out and thankfulness for his day. In the morning he awakes and prays a simple prayer (Help Me! Help Me! Help Me!). Keeping him focused on recovery and connected with God as he understands God. At the end of his day he then prays a second simple prayer (Thank You! Thank You! Thank You!). Keeping him aware that his simple prayer that morning was answered and he can rest easy during the night because he did his best and was not disconnected from the power of God as he understands God.

2. This author wakes up with a simple thought about what recovery means to him and reflects on it throughout the day. At the end of the day I recognize that recovery is tied to my self-awareness and connection to the world around me. Included in this process is a constant thoughtful focus on God as I understand God to be. To this day I continue to view recovery as connecting with God, allowing God to show me things to correct in my life and then following that direction.

3. Some use Guided meditation.

4. Still others use one of many different spiritual practices that are tied to cultural and religious practices.

This 3rd part in the opinion of many (this author included) is key to maintaining recovery as it gives purpose to life and keeps everything going so that all 3 parts of treatment are continually being worked on.

The process is not done when completed (Working the steps, Connection – Correction – Direction or however you define it) for it simply is part of growing and living the best today possible.

So now what? How can we work the Program? What is the process taken for Connection – Correction – Direction?

ACTIVITY SECTION

What Hit Home?

Consider what has been read and take time to 'digest' it. Now use this designated page to write down your thoughts.

CONNECTION!

In Recovery everything starts with connection. In the 12 steps it is steps 1, 2 and 3. In other programs it is demonstrated in the same manner if not the same 3 steps so let it begin here.

Step 1: We admitted we were powerless (over our addiction) that our lives had become unmanageable.

What does this look like? How did you experience this? For some it is the bottom of a deep hole, rock bottom or even "the end of the line". In these moments the desire to stop is strongest which opens up the opportunity to take the first step.

Starting the process is getting through the door of change regardless of what it looks like. That door of change could be anything from a 12 step meeting to a counselor OR even a moment of honesty with someone close to you. This reality is the beginning of recovery in part because it presents the choice to change or go back into the addict life.

The realization that something isn't quite right and life seems lost brings about the first step. Sadly it may be a step that is repeated many times before finally getting some solid footing. It may also arrive and take hold but as time passes a new addiction comes around.

Admitting powerlessness presents an opportunity to consider that there is a power that can help. It leads into step 2.

Step 2: Came to believe that a power greater than ourselves could restore us to a normal way of thinking and living.

This can be a difficult realization. As an addict all I thought of is how I could do what I wanted. Recovery shattered the illusion and left me seeking answers. When walking into the first meeting, counseling session, court hearing, family intervention etc. there often seems apprehension. The question is why am I here? Despite the Realization that I am powerless it may not sink in immediately. That simple realization in step 1 leads to seeking help beyond individual ability. That becomes a belief that there has to be more.

Step 3: Made a decision to turn our will and our lives over to the care of this Power of our own understanding.

Having seen the problem in step 1, considered and found belief in something greater than self (step 2) we turn over control to something greater than self (Step 3). Thus we begin connection.

Connection is realizing the simplest of ideas demonstrated by the statements below:

1. I fall down (did it my own way), we get back up (working on living as a part of community).

2. "Alone we can do so little; together we can do so much." – Helen Keller
3. Tell me and I forget. Teach me and I remember. Involve me and I learn. -Benjamin Franklin

4. What we can't do alone, we can do together.

Each quote has a key component of the process of connection. Individually it is easier to keep going in addiction but together it is worth making a change. An amazing transition comes out in one of the quotes though.

Benjamin Franklin transforms the process with a little twist. First is "Tell me and I forget." Which is very telling.

Remember when someone told you what to do? How likely is it that you wouldn't do what you were told? Growing up I remember being told to do something. When I questioned it and asked why I was told "because I said so". Being told what to do can easily be discounted and forgotten.

Next is "Teach me and I will remember". In school and in life being taught something (especially for a test) usually made it important enough to remember it long enough to pass the test or get through a situation. It really had little value beyond simply getting through the situation that I needed to know the information for.

Finally the key comes through with the last part. "Involve me and I learn.' Doing something as part of a group connects me with the process. Being included in an activity creates a sense of accomplishment. Connection is the beginning of progress.

So in Recovery connection is important. The 12 Step program addresses it in the first 3 steps. In contrast to that some use their faith or finding a community of faith to begin and still others connect with a counselor to work on the underlying issues to begin the process. Regardless of the way a person gets this first part of the process started it is focused on the same simple concept.

In addiction a person has connection with the disease but less so with others. They may even (often do) have some level of resentment toward those who try to tell them they have a problem and need help. Addiction is disconnection from others and the first step of recovery is to make connection with others.

Finding Connection allows for moving forward in small steps to fixing broken connections. This is the correction part of the 12 Step program (Steps 4, 5, 6, 7, 8 and 9).

ACTIVITY SECTION

What Hit Home?

Consider what has been read and take time to 'digest' it. Now use this designated page to write down your thoughts.

CORRECTION

Having made connection, however minimal at first, recovery has more work because connections are stronger when the past has been exercised and what created resentment is processed. The harm of the addiction needs to be addressed with some level of clarity. This is the next part of the process.

Correction is a process that has many different forms to work on it. The 12 Step programs use 6 of the steps to do this (Step 4, 5, 6, 7, 8 and 9). We will begin there with respect to working correction.

Step 4: Made a searching and fearless moral and financial inventory of ourselves.

This has been interpreted as a 'deep' dive into every aspect of life with the critical eye of a judge by some. By others it is seen as 'soul searching'. Both start with the thought that it is all about finding every wrong thing done and judging themselves.

Consider this idea for step 4: Looking at what has been a moral or financial problem in the past and how we need to change today.

Yes we are aware of the past but instead of using it to judge it becomes a process of making a course correction. In doing this we look at things with a fearless perspective. Identifying past mistakes, accepting that I am responsible for them and then looking at how to change myself to avoid repeating the wrongs of the past.

Step 5: Admitted to ourselves and to another human being the exact nature of our wrongs.

Having done step 4 with an understanding that change is needed (in the process taking personal responsibility) we admit to ourselves the problem.

Hence why Step 5 is more about finding a trusted person to share them with including how we see them (the exact nature of our wrongs). In many cases it is to get an objective view of the situation because working recovery sometimes clouds our view. Sharing it can clear up the difference between what we see and what is objectively the case.

Having someone to talk to with about this can help determine things like potential harm to others and how to approach making the correction needed.

Step 6: Were entirely ready to have these defects of character removed.

Because we shared in step 5 we may have a better clarity as to who we need to make amends to and how our 'character defects' played a role.

Step 6 is clearing away the clouds and filters blocking change. Once we can see clearer it is easier to desire change which is the process of dealing with defects of character.

For example: knowing that we have a tendency to behave negatively in a situation allows us to be ready to make changes. ("Be ready to have these defects of character removed".)

Step 7: Humbly asked God (of our understanding) to remove our shortcomings.

The course correction continues with step 7. Because we started this process with connection and became aware that alone we could not manage life, step 7 reminds us to ask for help. If I am going to change I need to be connected with life so that I have others who can provide perspective.

It is here that the connections made in steps 1, 2 and 3 become pertinent to making change. Consider how this looks to you. For myself and many others it is to ask for a spiritual being which passes beyond human understanding to help.

Step 8: Made a list of all persons we had harmed and became willing to make amends to them all

Step 8 takes everything done in earlier steps and allows for a sensible list to be made of people and organizations that were harmed. Without clarity this could become very overwhelming and provide a reason to avoid taking action.

Having gone through the steps to get to this point, we become willing to make amends. The areas where harm was done provide a starting point.

Step 9: Made direct amends to such people wherever possible, except when to do so would injure them or others.

Now we are at a place to take action with some clarity. The insight gained allows for consideration of how amends can be done without making things worse. That said it is always wise to have someone like in step 5 to process this with. Just because the clouds are clearing doesn't mean that our emotions don't cloud the process. With the help of someone who is objective, this process can be more sensitive to potential harm to others. It will allow for careful actions rather than making amends with the same expediency used when active in our addiction.

Because this process is likely one we will do for the rest of our lives amends can be done as we heal throughout life. The key part of recovery can now be approached now because a solid foundation and frame is in place.

ACTIVITY SECTION

What Hit Home?

Consider what has been read and take time to 'digest' it. Now use this designated page to write down your thoughts.

DIRECTION!

So now comes the work of taking time to 'smell the roses" and take action with a level of personal satisfaction. We have begun cleaning up our past by seeing change in the present.

Step 10: Continued to take personal inventory and when we were wrong, promptly admitted it.

Because being human is to make mistakes and be imperfect it is important to take time to evaluate our behavior daily (or at least very regularly).

Step 10 is simply a reminder to remain aware of what we are doing. Accept that while our addiction may be in remission with respect to the form that we started with, we can easily end up with a new form that may need to be treated.

Regular checkups are needed not only to prevent our past form of disease from returning but also to keep new forms from growing.

Step 11: Sought through prayer and meditation to improve our conscious contact with God as we understood Him, praying only for knowledge of His will for us and the power to carry that out.

In recovery it may well be the most important step that we see here. Prayer and meditation is an act of connecting with a part of life that is often left to sit quietly in a corner until we get in trouble.

Step 11 is recognition that it should be ongoing, front and center, in daily life. Regardless of how you define the organized and real world (Nature, Creation, God) being connected with it is key. In the disease we may have cried out when we needed a win or the answer to how to keep our addiction from damaging a relationship. In recovery we have the chance to change from crying out to communicating with.

It is at this place in the 12 Steps that a change in how we respond becomes an option. The opportunity is to simply have a conversation with rather than a conversation at.

So focusing on asking and then listening for the answer allows for change. In this the change is seeking an answer when we used to force the answer we wanted.

This can change a person in ways that allow visible changes in how the world looks. It can lead to action which is where the 12th step takes over.

Step 12: Having made an effort to practice these principles in all our affairs, we tried to carry this message to other compulsive gamblers.

Early in recovery this was straight forward for me. I have principles that are recovery and now I need to carry the recovery message to others with the voracity of a "Hell Fire and Brimstone" preacher.

Now it is less clear in that sense but clearer than any direct message sent with force. It is here that the foundation and walls of my recovery home are built and it is time to 'move in' to the new home.

Recovery is making an effort to live life in all the ways it was meant to be. Practicing the steps in all my affairs is living life, being present with people who were not part of the gambling but are part of my life. Things I missed or was only there physically when in my addiction are now things I don't miss. In doing this the message is carried to everyone without respect to if they are an addict or a person in my life.

Anger may crop up but it is no longer about covering up the addiction because I can see the situation rather than the obstacle to going back.

Having covered the 12 Steps as a form of recovery rather than the actual program, I can build my life as a home. Recovery as a program is a journey defined by CCD (connection – Correction – Direction). It is a program that can be worked with 12 steps, 3 parts of active change or even simply accepting help when I fall down. In the next few pages think about the pictures and see if you can see recovery in them.

ACTIVITY SECTION

What Hit Home?

Consider what has been read and take time to 'digest' it. Now use this designated page to write down your thoughts.

THE DESTINATION

Having recovery is different from having abstinence. Since it is more than the 12 Steps and is personal it seems reasonable to share thoughts and ideas from my personal journey.

- I am a recovering Addict.
- I have an addiction that presented as Gambling but can present itself in other ways if I am not aware.
- For me there is a huge difference between accepting I have something and I am something.

When this book started it was about the shattered life of addiction. Moving forward it became about a fractured recovery process and how to work through it.

Now what??

Well it might be good to look at what was and see what is. In looking at this what can be become possible. No longer is it "Hopeless", "Religion" or "The 12 Step Program".

If it isn't any of this then what could it be?

It probably is something that ties things together in a process that is connected. The idea of connection – correction – Direction leads somewhere and while everything up to this point has been a step toward a destination it doesn't stop there. Recovery is a fluid process with a moving destination for growth. Each day presents its own new arrival which is a destination along the way to what is yet to be.

Recovery begins with where we are and not with where we were and definitely not with where we assume or expect to be.

Addiction is a disease of symptoms which may explain why some avoid recognizing them. The treatment begins focused on the specific form and what the causes are for the symptoms.

Recovery starts in realizing the problem. Sometimes others see the symptoms first and other times the person with them notices.

The symptoms

1. An inability to stop
2. Use continues despite health problems
3. Avoiding dealing with problems
4. Obsession to the exclusion of all else
5. Taking risks
6. Sacrifices
7. Dropping hobbies and activities
8. Secrecy and solitude
9. Denial & rationalizing one's poor choices or harmful behavior
10. Legal issues
11. Financial difficulties
12. Withdrawal symptoms
13. Appetite changes
14. Damage or disease
15. Sleeplessness
16. A change in one's physical appearance or personality
17. Increasing tolerance

Definition

The definition of Addiction: an inability to stop using a substance or engaging in a behavior even though it is causing psychological and physical harm.

Digging into the general definition shows that the disease is less in the form of the addiction but rather the amount of use causing symptoms. Regardless of whether it is a substance, behavior or activity the disease develops in the excessive involvement.

The 17 listed symptoms are seen differently depending on the form that addiction presents.

Symptoms Discussed

An inability to stop:

The first symptom is an inability to stop which by itself seems mild. At first it may seem to be more of the desire to complete a task so it can seem like a good thing. The problem comes when it goes beyond completing a task. Workaholics are a good example because when it starts it may be simply seen as good work ethic. Few people start a project and don't finish it as promptly as they can. If it is one that takes several weeks then the person focuses on it at work until it is completed.

In the case of a workaholic when the task is done they take little time to breathe before starting the next task. Once started even the end of the scheduled work day may be overlooked to keep going. The set schedule with its breaks may simply be ignored to the exception of the job.

Most addictions are like this. Stopping is not likely until the person is unable to continue for any number of reasons (no more money, someone with them pulls them away, simple exhaustion).

Use continues despite health problems

Continuing active addiction even if a health problem is present is not uncommon. Consider the person with liver disease who continues to drink or the over eater who continues to eat despite continuing weight gain. Is the disease stopped by that? No.

As a recovering compulsive Gambler, I can say that even having a severe sinus infection, the Flu or any number of other issues were no reason to stop gambling. I can also say that bladder issues didn't stop me from drinking excessive amounts of Mountain Dew. I had to have severe breathing issues to stop smoking but all I did is found something else to replace smoking.

Most addicts I have met are so focused on the addiction that even if a Doctor made clear they had to stop before it killed them they would keep going.

Avoiding dealing with problems

How we deal with problems is a key symptom. As an addict I went to the addiction to avoid actually dealing with a problem. Avoiding the real problem for a while was a solution but all that really happened is finding the problem was worse.

Reality check... Addicts avoid facing problems and as a result the problem only gets worse.

Obsession to the exclusion of all else

The avoidance of problems is really more of an obsession with the addiction. No matter how bad it gets the next time will help make it better. Getting money to keep going with the obsession is key to getting better. This becomes a big lie for the addict because it only gets worse. It is also an extension of the avoidance into an over compensation to escape

Taking risks:

Because the addict can't stop, is not deterred by health or problems and it becomes an obsession and their self-destructive behavior is risk driven. Addiction becomes a 'challenge' to see how long they can continue. Things like work and sleep may become so disconnected that the addiction continues with potential consequences.

Sacrifices

This one is a bit harder to see as it is often done in ways that people do not realize it. The addiction takes over to the point that time with others, work and activities that used to be important are sacrificed or simply abandoned to make room to nurture the addiction. Often it is intermingled with the other symptoms and not seen for the 'forest of' surface level indications. The addiction is done to the exclusion of healthy eating and medical care. Both of these are symptoms of the disease but who considers the results of those symptoms which are actually sacrifices for the sake of the addiction?

Dropping hobbies and activities

Dropping hobbies and activities is fairly obvious but can also be seen as substituting a hobby or activity with the addiction as a new one (in the case of process/ behavioral addictions).

The big substitutions are when it becomes more obvious. For example missing family events (birthdays, retirement parties and family gatherings) is where it becomes very clear.

Secrecy and solitude

Addiction is a solitary activity and often the addict knows that it will present problems especially when they start to run out of excuses and they fear being exposed. So they continue to come up with more and more elaborate excuses and being secretive about the true details. An addict will eventually retreat into solitude as doing so provides them with the opportunity to feed their urges without having someone there trying to 'fix' them. Creating arguments can provide the solitude and distance from others. Basically disconnecting to allow hiding that what is really going on. It is easier to keep a secret if you don't have people around you.

Denial & rationalizing one's poor choices or harmful behavior

This symptom is fairly easy as it becomes visible when confronted by someone. Ask any addict if they have a problem with... and the answer often will be no because the addict in active addiction still holds the skewed belief that they have things under control. It becomes yet another reason to avoid facing the addiction. It is the easiest thing for someone to do when asked about it. The big problem is that this denial is more than about the addiction.

The denial is relative to every reason for being active in the addiction. It is about what is being avoided, dealt with, treated or almost anything that has led to active addiction. Reality is not the same for the addict as it is for everyone around them. The addiction becomes often a form of 'self-medication' that the addict rationalizes as something they need to feel better or help them cope.

Legal and Financial difficulties:

Because life is unmanageable for an addict it leads to issues with the law and /or financial problems. The most obvious are the people who have gotten DUI's, been arrested for committing a crime or even being admitted involuntarily to a mental health facility.

Less obvious are the legal issues a person gets in with themselves. Stealing from their bill money, Overdrafts and other internal conflicts. Often the internal legal and financial issues revolve around the self-image a person has. It may not even be recognized by the addict but they ruin their reputation with themselves. The way they look at and value themselves is a reflection of personal reputation.

There is also the component of low self-esteem where addicts on a subconscious level do not believe they are worthy of having success or good things in life. Having a career, a good paying job or coming into money affords one with personal freedoms and feeling accomplished. Similarly, developing and maintaining positive connections with others brings one joy, where such positive emotions the addict does not believe they are worthy of or deserving to experience. This negative self-depravity lays the ideal foundation for the addiction to take root and progressively continue on with its goal to destroy the addict until there is truly nothing left for them to lose.

Withdrawal symptoms:

If the addict is far enough along it becomes obvious when they are unable to actively participate in the addiction. Basically an addict who can't partake will become very unpredictable and may even beg others to help them.

What can be seen both as the addiction gets worse and as they start recovery is strong evidence of the addiction's hold.

The addict demonstrates:

1. **Appetite changes**: This can be eating more or less, healthier or unhealthy. In the addiction this may be demonstrated by the addiction replacing meals and in recovery it can be eating more. It may be obvious or minute. The key is that the habits are changed. Sadly it can be an effect of the addiction or tied to other symptoms.

2. **Damage or disease**: This symptom is often a direct response to the addiction itself. Things like Cancer due to smoking or other environmental aspects of an addiction are examples. Parkinson's, Brain defects, nervous system damage and so many other things are potentially a result of the addiction. Withdrawal can also create a problem as the body becomes acclimated to the addiction and when it is removed the body has damage as a result of the recovery.

3. **Sleeplessness**: With addiction it depends on the form it takes but in many cases it is not uncommon for a person to have difficulty sleeping. The addiction becomes an all-encompassing focus and every waking hour is looking for the next high or opportunity to be numb. The agitation of withdrawal also keeps the person awake. Recovery starts when the anxiety of withdrawal makes sleep a foreign concept. The problem is that because everyone is different it is also possible that the person sleeps more rather than being awake.

A change in one's physical appearance or personality

Addiction can easily become a case where the disease takes over all aspects of self-care. As a result the person may lack normal care that most people do as a part of everyday routine. Common things as listed below are potential signs of the addiction.

  a. Weight gain or loss due to changes in eating habits or simply not eating at all in favor of the addiction of choice.
  b. Lack of bathing due to a focus on the addiction without concern for cleaning up. This may be noted even by smell or greasy hair etc.

Addiction also changes the individual's personality over time. As the disease ravages and progressively continues to destroy important elements of one's life, the individual becomes increasingly stressed over their losses. Their emotional state becomes impacted resulting in a change in how they respond to particular situations and how they interact with others. Examples of personality changes can include:

  a. Reactive and easily frustrated
  b. Angers easily including being verbally abusive and /or becoming physically abusive
  c. Withdrawn
  d. Disinterested or phlegmatic
  e. Depressed
  f. Super sensitive
  g. Paranoid
  h. Affect to situational context is often mismatched or inappropriate (e.g., appear sad during a joyous celebration or alternatively laugh or make jokes during a serious discussion)

Increasing tolerance

An addict has the desire for increasing use because as the body gets used to the addiction the original emotional or physical high from the addiction wanes. So the addict increases use in an attempt to produce the same effect the addiction delivered in the beginning.

Unfortunately attempts to use more just moves the goal post of the expected and desired outcome as the addiction intensifies.

This is easiest explained with pain medications. Someone with chronic pain and taking pain medicine to alleviate their pain finds that their pain increases over time and thus the medication no longer has the same therapeutic effect of alleviating their pain. As a result the dosage may be increased.

The same happens with addicts but with the twist that the addict may reach a point where the desired results are not reached and the chase ends up going beyond the level that the body can process. At this point it can lead to an overdose. Withdrawal is dangerous as it creates stronger desire to stop the pain caused by it. As a result if a person relapses it may be a fatal outcome.

The last one is something to be especially aware of as it is a danger with relapse. Over time increasing tolerance for the addiction creates stronger dependence and higher danger for the addiction to cause death with relapses. The further into recovery a person gets the more dangerous it gets. With the addiction leaving the person's physical system, the tolerance can go down and yet a relapse can present as if it hasn't gone down. The person believes they need more because the tolerance was such that it took more at the end. When a relapse happens it may well be deadly because the person still believes the higher amount will be needed. The higher level then becomes so dangerous that it may kill the first time.

So what is the destination? It is the constant move toward living life better today. The destination is ahead of people in recovery and not as important as the journey which is found in daily life.

Recovery Moves Forward

While many find recovery using the set structure of 12 step programs/ the Anonymous fellowships, it is not the only way to look at recovery. Much like different languages use different words/ characters/ alphabets that say the same thing in a different way, recovery is the same at the foundation but looks different for each person.

Through the process of this book we have seen the program through different eyes and defined with different words/ steps. Even with the different views one thing remained at the core. That core is about change from past to being different. Moving forward in recovery is not about how it is defined by some person but rather by a natural process of human nature and a desire to have connection with the world around us.

Personality based recovery can be seen in the view of:

1. Hopeless
2. Religion

A merging of personality and principle can be seen in:

1. The 12 Step Program

In reality the foundation of principles is in that core where the other views are based:

1. I Fall Down… We Get Back Up
2. Connection – Correction – Direction

Here in lies the problem of life: being human it is not possible to be emotionless, reaction free and stoic. The principles at the core are hard and in the history of humanity there have not been too many that lived fully by the principles without faltering. Life is not about perfectly principled living but in improving principled living each day.

Living the foundation aspect is knowing that mistakes are a part of life but they are not the end of living.

Core principles explained:

I Fall Down… We Get Back Up

Falling down is a process each person does on their own and is demonstrated in many ways. To live with this principle it is necessary to accept help.

The disease of addiction is personally owned but the treatment is allowing others to be a part of helping me up. It is in being willing to believe in a power that you cannot see but can experience that connection with society is found.

Connection – Correction – Direction

The core of recovery is in the principle of process. The addiction is about the person. Disease is within and apart from life. The process begins with allowing it to be about connecting with everything and everyone in the world around us.
The 3 parts of this principle can be broken down like this:

Connection

Getting past the self-involved process and allowing for it to be about finding a place to "fit in" and be part of society. As discussed earlier it all starts with admitting, believing and committing. Admitting that alone I fall. Believing that it is possible to achieve more with help. Committing to making a connection with both people I see and what I cannot see in the environment around me (God).

Correction

After going through the process of connecting it becomes necessary to look at what needs to change for successful living. This involves reviewing what I did in the past and considering ways to change from the reactive past to a proactive nature. As mentioned earlier it involves taking an honest inventory. Being courageous enough to look at things objectively to learn from the past. Repairing relationships from the past when possible and letting go when it is not possible.

Direction

Finally the process of evaluation begins because letting go of power (Connection) and taking stock in what happened in the past (Correction) have been instilled into the healing process. The question becomes "What Now?"

In the past I was comfortable with 'self medicating" and living with a belief of having control. This can't be taken forward though because now life includes affecting others. Life is no longer about me and what I want but rather about life and what I need to be living to the best of what is possible as part of a bigger picture.

To answer the question takes patience and willingness to listen. Some meditate, others pray and still others simply take time to sit quietly. All of this is the same thing. It is seeking direction by allowing for peaceful flow of life to give guidance.

By allowing for a time of seeking perspective on what the day can be and remembering that it is more than simply doing what I want, life changes. At the end of the day time can be taken to assess what has passed (Review Connection and correction).

Even as direction is sought it is important to remember that being human means that personalities, emotions and nature affect the process. It is not about the destination but about the realization that the journey is more than what was. It is in what is and is yet to be.

The destination is both in getting up and going to bed. The final destination (end of life) is not something to dwell on as it will come when it comes. All that matters is where we are right now.

ACTIVITY SECTION

What Hit Home?

Consider what has been read and take time to 'digest' it. Now use this designated page to write down your thoughts.

Final Thoughts

Up to this point it has been about a process that talks of being broken and finding some level of healing that puts things back together. At least to a point of functional survival.

Now to something a bit more personal than simply telling a story or explaining a personal view. As stated at the beginning of this process there is a personal experience that takes place. It is my hope that in sharing what is written others will hear the message below as a final note to recovery.

It is my heart and mind that sees life as a part of something bigger. Recovery begins with a shattered person with life in pieces so broken that it feels hopeless. It moves to finding a small light of hope that brings healing into the view of possibility. It may stop there with connection to others with similar struggles. It can be more than simply putting structure to the vessel of life and that is where recovery becomes living a full life.

For the first few years simply finding a group that understood me and knew what I was fighting each day was enough. Then came the following realizations that what I was and understanding what I went through was not enough. What I came to discover was the following:
- I was in pain and I can relate to what was but recovery is more to me.
- It is what I am becoming and what I am now that matters most.
- I don't want to go back and I don't want to sweep it away.
- I can't fully understand people who went through the same disease of gambling addiction because their journey had different things that happened in different ways.
- I understand the disease and the pain but like genetics makes each person unique so it is with addiction.
- The disease is the same but it is unique in how it attacks each unique individual. It has no preference as to income, color, race, gender, age or any other distinguishing factor that makes a person who they are.
- Addiction simply grows where it finds a viable host.

Addiction is not defined by the form it takes except for by those who battle it in the light of their experience. Recovery is however defined by how it is seen by those who see a loved one once believed lost, people who meet the addict in recovery and see who they are rather than who they were and then as a result by the person experiencing recovery.

What we have lived in addiction has common connection but not always common journey. In the simplest of terms addiction is addiction. It does not truly matter if it is Gambling, Drugs, Alcohol or any of the many forms it comes in. Initially it may be targeted with both its formation and its treatment but ultimately the disease destroys the host. It doesn't destroy one part of the 'host' (liver, stomach, Leg etc.) Addiction regardless of form results in 3 things all of which boil down to one final outcome…Death. This is the core of addiction while the form is a 'venue' or starting point to achieve the end results.

The "prison, Insanity or Death" outcome stated for all 12 step programs seems to be superficial as in reality death comes in many forms and three of them are listed in the statement.

Prison is a stage of death of addicts. It often leads to the death of employment, death of relationships and death of self integrity if nothing changes. This stage has some hope of coming back to life in society but only if the addict is willing.

Insanity is also a stage of death. Without clear thought it could be considered 'Brain dead". Again the form of death is not permanent as it is possible to get treatment and return to society.

Finally there is the final and direct form. In this case returning is either impossible of very unlikely. Death in the most permanent form results in taking all the wreckage left behind and spreading it to all who are still alive.

These 3 are all given connection to every form of addiction that has a 12 step program associated with it. If this is the case then it is not about the form but rather the 'prognosis' (outcome). There are 3 potential outcomes that have been seen each a result of how treatment is done.

3 Outcomes of Addiction

The outcomes are not the ones given above (Prison, Insanity or Death), they are more pragmatic (Practical).

Outcome 1: Death

This is a permanent outcome that eliminates the host form existence. The progress is part of the progressively worse idea of 12 step programs. This outcome has no future to be seen and will forever leave destruction as the defining legacy.

Outcome 2: Abstinence/ Stagnant Existence

Many are here because it is where addiction in one or more forms ends but replacement is a constant part of the process.

With abstinence comes limited treatment. The person treats the addiction they see but does not monitor for new forms that present.

It leaves room for transferring from one form to another. Examples are gambling stops but drinking, drugs, eating, smoking or any of thousands of other forms start. One of the most common forms to fill the void is something that seems very innocent and is seldom seen due to the nature of it.

The helper who goes beyond simply being of service. Not all such situations are bad but it is important to remember the very first steps of recovery to avoid it. If not the feelings of self-importance, being put on a pedestal and other such things can become addictive as well. When a person or group of people become so important that others are willing to listen blindly to them or consider them to 'have all the answers they need it becomes a power and control environment waiting to happen.

Abstinence can work for a time but if it is where the recovery remains then it is prone to relapse and/ or addiction substitution.

Outcome 3: Full Remission treatment

This process a person starts with the addiction that is presenting and treats it directly and then as time passes they begin to do reviews of the process. It involves the intensive treatment which is seen with abstinence but at some point goes into a screening process. Much like cancer treatments which targets the disease where it is to get it into remission as the starting point. Once remission is achieved the treatment goes into a maintenance stage.

Once the original form is in remission the process goes into regular checkups in this process the checkups are more than checking the original location. It involves checking for any sign of cancer through blood tests and other forms of monitoring.

With addiction it would be taking care of the primary form (Gambling, Alcohol, Drugs, Food and others) to maintain control of that first. Once it is in a level of remission the work goes to seeing if there are other forms that have come in to replace it and/ or there were co-occurring forms such as smoking.

Recovery is not something that will be completely finished while alive because as humans we have a natural draw toward addictive things. Sometimes they are so minor that they do not affect life but other times they are debilitating.

People Growing Hope & Recovery considers the potential to become addicted to anything to the exclusion of everything else. The only way to treat such a 'potential' may well be to find the potential of life as a counter balance. A higher power, regardless of how it is seen gives balance.

A New Form Of Sponsorship

Over the years recovery in the 12 step programs focused on the concept of sponsoring relationships. As time has progressed so has this concept. It has been the home of both good and bad things. PGHR looks at this as a different process.

Since every member has considered the first 3 steps and in doing so seen that there is a greater power than self/ individual, PGHR has considered the concepts of Recovery as a lifelong Pilgrimage with periods of Sojourning.

Pilgrimage: a personal journey especially a sacred personal life style change. The course of life in recovery on earth.

Sojourning: This is when a person (or group) is sitting together, either for a set time, in a place that is not involving the comfort of past addiction and is dependent on the willingness of the fellowship to work for a common process of learning a new way to live.

This recovery process focuses on 3 territories that are visited regularly as part of the Pilgrimage.

Pilgrimage stop 1: where recovery works on Connection.

1. Sojourning to see admitted problems that are not manageable (Step 1).

2. Sojourning to find belief in something greater than self that can help with the problem (step 2).

3. Sojourning to accepting the will of a greater power by handing over personal will power in favor of the greater power (Step 3).

Pilgrimage stop 2: where we are guided to make changes (Correction)

1) Sojourning into a personal inventory of life. Taking a fearless moral and financial inventory of all aspects. (Step 4).

2) Sojourning into admitting to ourselves and to another human being the exact nature of our wrongs (as we see them) (Step 5).

3) Sojourning into willing to let that power remove defects of character (step 6).

4) Sojourning humbly asked that power to remove our defects of character (step 7).

5) Sojourning to list of all persons we had harmed with a willingness to make amends (step 8).

6) Sojourning to make direct amends wherever possible, except when to do so would injure any or all involved persons (step 9).

Pilgrimage stop 3:

1) Sojourning: to take personal inventory continually and when wrong, promptly admit it (step 10).

2) Sojourning through prayer and meditation to improve our conscious contact with that greater power (as we understand it), praying only for knowledge of our purpose and the power to carry that out (with help) (step 11).

3) Sojourning to make an effort to practice these principles in all areas of our life, continuing to do our best to carry this message to others by word and action (step 12).

Continuing The Pilgrimage With Daily Sojourning

Some might think that once done it is not necessary to continue from the beginning of the steps/ journey as listed. In some ways that is correct but in reality it is necessary to keep repeating the process as each time it is not from the same place. For the Pilgrimage is lifelong and always moving forward. It is not that the sojourns are repeated but that they are made in a new place along the pilgrimage. Each stop is exploring a new 'territory'. Recovery starts with a small seed and grows over time.

Now to the progress of life from Broken Addict to Fractured Recovery and what comes next?

The Closing

When this book started we were talking about the shattered life of an addict regardless of the form it took. Like a Glass cup that has been shattered into a million pieces a person comes to the point where everything is a mess and it is nearly impossible to see any use. This is where change begins.

From that mess a solution is sought for the single addiction that we see. Working the 'program' with others who have the same problem (or appear to have the same problem on the surface). From the shattered million piece mess a start. Recovery begins with intensive work to put things back together and visually things look good. Most people stop there and accept the way it is. Some end up finding a new form of addiction and repeat the process with people of the same type. Others simply end up back to the old ways and reliving 'day one' over and over.

Now consider this idea: what if you didn't stop with the surface? Instead keep going as a lifelong pilgrimage and focus on seeing beyond addiction to continual self growth.

I found simply getting better and not being active in my known addiction was not enough for me. I still had life events that created pain and led to escape. 4 years into the process, sitting in a hospital I found myself asking why.

I found direction in that moment which is why I accept that I am a human with emotions and addictions to more than what I could see. It was in my genetics and the only way to get better was to face being flawed with principles that are the core were of making change.

Life is for living and if the focus is on what was and constant review then today becomes a shadow of living.

Here are 21 principles to live by and rather than focusing on those who have the 'same problem", I look at people who are working the same solution and willing to balance life so that it becomes a more fulfilling life.

PRINCIPLES OF RECOVERY AND LIFE:

1) **Confidentiality** – Live to maintain the confidence of others at all times.
2) **Competence** Live to represent the community with a high level of competence in the process of learning to live.
3) **Community Courtesy** Live to treat others with fairness and courtesy.
4) **Trust** – Live to instill a sense of trust in those around you.
5) **Do No Harm** Live to avoid any activity that would cause harm to others.
6) **Privacy** Live to avoid sharing the details of others past histories, present struggles or present life events without their advance consent or expressed permission.
7) **Integrity** – Live in a way that maintains honesty and clear communication in all areas of live.
8) **Teamwork** – Live to work together to learn, grow and accomplish a better way of life.
9) **Objectivity** –Live without making decisions based on whom I like best or with whom I have a personal relationship. Rather, make decisions based on the ability demonstrated
10) **Consideration** – Live to put the needs of others first whenever possible when it does not affect my own need for growth.
11) **Growth** – Live to to pursue personal growth rather than that of everyone else's expectations.

12) **Communication** – Live to work with others as a support for each other. This entails learning to actively listen to others so I may better understand and appreciate their unique situation.

13) **Respect** – Live to respect people's boundaries, choices and lives including my own.

14) **Loyalty** – Live to put family and friends' needs before my own whenever possible.

15) **Honesty** – Live to be honest with myself and to speak truthfully and respectfully. When I realize I was/ am wrong admit it to others immediately.

16) **Pursue Peace** – Live to avoid violence in all cases!

17) **Forgiveness** - Live to find it in my heart to let go and move forward from past hurts that others caused me. Forgiveness does not require forgetting what I went through. Rather, the ability to release the pain from my heart as well as the individual who did me wrong to a higher power.

18) **Reserve Judgement** – Live to let go of judgement. I may never know all the reasons or life circumstances that contributed or led someone to make poor decisions, or to do something that I do not agree with. Instead of judging someone on their past actions look to how they have grown and the way their past shaped their present character.

19) **Sustainable Living** - Live in a way that doesn't waste what I have available.

20) **Care for the Vulnerable** – Live to care for those who are struggling, may be vulnerable or at risk of being manipulated by others. At the same time, caring for others needs to be balanced so that by helping others is not to my own or to my loved one's detriment.

21) **Benefit the Greater Good** – Live to make sure that my decisions to help others is not self-serving.

ACTIVITY SECTION

What Hit Home?

Consider what has been read and take time to 'digest' it. Now use this designated page to write down your thoughts.

Finally, I thought it would be relevant to also provide another perspective that ties in with the information shared in this book on how some other addiction recovery experts have come to identify addiction as a "SYMPTOM" of an underlying root cause rather than viewing addiction as the problem to treat.

In the next part of this book, Remedy Max, the founder of Fractured Psyche Addiction Recovery Model details what behavior addictions actually represent. She also explains how early exposure to traumatic life events can contribute to an individual developing an addiction, what the driving force behind their addiction of preference entails and also what steps are needed to end the cycle of relapse by working on healing one's injured mind to reclaim one's life back.

About Remedy Max, MA, BA, DRI-ABCP

Remedy Max is a published author, safety & security columnist, professional public speaker and subject matter expert on social, situational and environmental risk mitigation and prevention.

She holds a BA (Hons.) degree in Criminology, Law & Ethics, Bioethics and a Master's degree in Criminology and Collaborative Behavior / Substance Abuse & Addictions Studies from the University of Toronto in Canada. In addition she holds numerous certifications in Human Behavior Sciences, Personality Disorders, Crime Prevention, Emergency Preparedness and Disaster Risk Management.

Over the past 20 years she has worked with domestic abuse survivors and those struggling with various behavior addictions like problem gambling to help guide them in their recovery. She is also an active member and advisor in PGHR and affiliate of many international organizations working towards enhancing public awareness about addiction, domestic abuse and intimate partner violence prevention, harm reduction & crime prevention as well as accessibility design for persons with disabilities.

Remedy Max is also the president & CEO of RemedyBlox, a company she founded in 2014 where she and her team of subject matter experts deliver proactive strategies aimed to guide members of the public and help the business sector recognize risks early on, to help them mitigate against various social, situational and environmental risks and losses.

The Fractured Psyche Addiction Recovery Model

By Remedy Max, MA, BA, DRI-ABCP

So What Exactly is the Fractured Psyche Addiction Recovery Model?

According to this recovery model, behavior addictions like problem gambling, compulsive shopping, eating disorders, workaholism, sex addiction, and many other self-destructive compulsions.are viewed as symptomatic expressions of the addict's subconscious mindset which was fractured by an earlier exposure to some traumatic life event(s) well before the individual's addiction reared its ugly head.

Traumatic life events can entail:

- Surviving domestic abuse / intimate partner violence

- Surviving a traumatic life changing accident,

- Being a victim of a violent assault,

- Having a loved one die suddenly,

- Battle with a serious health issue or dealing with a loved one's terminal illness,

- Having gone through a painful and difficult divorce, or

- Having experienced some form of physical, emotional and/or sexual childhood abuse, including

- Having endured other negative social / economic struggles during one's formative years.

Since traumatic life experiences (regardless of their severity or duration) are found in most if not among all addicts - the impact of such earlier trauma and their injurious lasting psychological effects on the individual's subconscious mindset (their psyche) cannot be discounted, minimized nor ignored when it comes to understanding addiction onset and the recovery process.

Under the revolutionary and progressive **"Fractured Psyche Addiction Recovery Model"** coined in the early part of 2000 by Remedy Max - the contention is that whenever the survivor of a traumatic life event fails to mentally process or properly heal psychologically from their past traumatic experience(s) (preferably under the guidance of a trained professional) - then the onset / development of a high risk behavior compulsion or substance abuse leading to a serious addiction is more likely to occur.

It is presumed that the reasons for this happening is attributed to when the trauma survivor relies on avoidance or minimization techniques as their way to cope with their pain instead of dealing and properly processing their past traumatic event(s).

Unfortunately when the individual does this, their injured psyche (their subconscious mind) is denied the opportunity to properly process and heal from the trauma it sustained.

Basically said, when the survivor the "individual self" does not offer crucial answers to their subconscious mind as to how and why the past traumatic event(s) happened - their subconscious mind will resort to conjuring up its own version of answers (in its limited form) so that the past can be processed and the psyche can find the needed closure to allow it to move on and function to its best ability.

During this time when the injured mind searches for answers and without any guidance or assistance received from the individual - the subconscious mind (psyche) of the individual ends up concluding that the events happened because of the individual "self's" shortcomings and inability to stop or prevent the earlier forms of trauma.

What is happening at this time as well is that the mind ends up blaming the "individual self" for the dire and painful past event(s) and no longer trusts or respects the individual.

During this process the individual's mind / psyche also proceeds to form a negative view about the "individual self" where the psyche comes to regard the "individual self" as being weak, inept and a failure that cannot be trusted - including deeming the individual self as being unworthy and undeserving to have anything good in their life now or in the future because of their prior inability to safeguard against past risk exposures or prevent bad things from happening.

When the subconscious mind conjures up such a negative narrative about their "individual self" (while limited and irrational) it comes to assert itself in control over the "individual self".

It is at that very moment that the fracture of the psyche is formed and it will do anything in its power to protect the negative view it formed and preventing it from becoming invalidated by the "individual self's" actions moving forward. In addition, the individual's fractured mind also is deeply angered and upset where it will seek to exact revenge as a retaliatory reaction for the pain and hurt it perceives resulted from the individual self's shortcomings when the individual failed to stop or prevent the traumatic life event(s) from happening in the past,

Meaning, after the traumic life event(s) have passed and the individual proceeds to move on with their life in a positive manner such as trying to find new happiness in life, become successful, start to feel good about themselves and achieve various accomplishments in life (e.g., securing a good paying job, owning a nice home, developing strong social support networks, finding a loving partner, getting married, having children, feeling at peace and in control over their life, etc..) their fractured psyche becomes alarmed and starts to look for ways to eliminate each of those positive and happy life milestone achievements that the individual has or is trying to accomplish. This process happens because the individual's fractured psyche sees these achievements as a threat and it is fearful that the negative narrative and view of the individual self it had formed before as a means to cope with the trauma is now at risk of being invalidated and devalued.

Using the **"Fractured Psyche Addiction Recovery Model"** the person battling behavior addiction(s) is guided to view their self-destructive compulsions as a symptom of the actual underlying problem. Through this recovery model the individual battling an addiction also comes to discover how their mind is working against them and that their psyche's fracture orchestrates the allure for high risk behaviors using deceptive tactics to get them to fall into the mindtrap over and over again to act on self-destructive urges that are carefully crafted to produce only dire outcomes which progress in intensity and severity over time seeking their ultimate and complete demise.

Unfortunately, those battling addictions who remain unaware of what their the fractured psyche is doing or what the gambling urges or any other high risk behavior temptations are all about, they will fall into the trap their fractured psyche presents. They will act on the presented alluring urges for self-destructive behavior find themselves over and over again as they see each aspect of their life become progressively destroyed not understanding why or how that could have happened.

For individuals who become compulsive gamblers - their fractured psyche presents gambling urges brimming with favorable possibilities and positive outcomes. Gambling is pitched as an opportunity to feel in control, to escape to a place that offers some form of enjoyment, to feel free, happy and achieve a sense of new found financial freedom that will afford one with better sense of security and more options in life.

Basically the problem gambler is misled by their fractured psyche over and over again - each time the gambling urges are presented.

For the problem gambler who remains unaware of the mental processes going on in the background, they will continue to buy into the skewed expectation that going to gamble at any means will eventually afford them with not just feeling good and in control in the moment while gambling but also the financial means and freedom to change their life and the life of those whom they care about for the better.

This illusive hope and anticipated outcome that a gambling win will change one's life for the better is most particularly appealing to the individual who has experienced a painful past, a significant or tragic loss or who had felt trapped, helpless, insecure or inept to escape, avoid or prevent an earlier traumatic life event from happening.

Given these contributing factors that lead an individual to gamble compulsively help dispel the common incorrect beliefs, misconceptions and negative social stigma held by some about problem gamblers. Often viewing problem gamblers as being selfish, lazy, deceitful, greedy individuals who have some moral defect to explain why they continue to gamble.

These negative assumptions and false stereotypes are simply inaccurate and serve no other purpose than to cast judgement that further erode the already low and diminshed sense of self-worth and a fragile state of mind of the problem gambler.

Instead, what actually needs to be recognized by all is the real motivational factors that underpin and lead problem gamblers to continue to continue to feed their gambling addiction. What needs to be realized is that gambling has nothing to do with greed or a moral defect. Rather compuslive gambling is attributed to how the addict's fractured psyche has found an effective way to get the individual self to punish themselves and to progressively lose everything that they have achieved in life to validate the negative narrative the fractured psyche formed.

Gambling is nothing more than the means with which the fractured mind can deny the individual self to feel a sense of joy and peace in life, and to get the individual to eliminate that which they value and hold dear - just so their fractured mind's negative view about them can continue to be validated over and over again with each gambling loss sustained.

Basically said, gambling urges are a carefully orchestrated ruse by the problem gambler's fractured psyche that creates false hopes and builds unattainable expectations.

The problem gambler is constantly misled into believing that gambling will yield a big enough win will empower them as well as afford them with financial opportunities to alleviate current struggles or mitigate against future hardships that life might present.

Unfortunately, little does the Problem Gambler realize early on that the real nefarious motives and timing with which the gambling urges are presented by their fractured psyche. Urges are all about getting them to destroy their financial security, social connections to others, and their personal freedom and choices in life,

The fractured psyche is also very cunning and it does its best to not tip its hand to the individual self about what it's motivations are or when urges for self-destructive behaviors are pitched to the unsuspecting addict,.

The following examples help illustrate when and how gambling urges are typically presented by the individual's fractured psyche to achieve least resistance and maximum buy-in by the individual:

POSITIVE LIFE EVENTS

The "individual self" is feeling good about themselves or that which they have recently accomplished in their life such as:

- Coming into money (eg. getting pad at work or for a job performed or selling something of value)

- Securing a job/career that one feels good doing

- Owning a nice home,

- Having strong healthy relationships with others,

- Entering addiction recovery

- Having achieved a milestone in recovery time

- Successfully reducing one's debt load

- Securing a consolidation loan to ease financial stress

- Remortgaging one's home

- Going on a well deserved relaxing vacation

- Planning a wedding

- Birth of a child

All of these positive life achievements pose a direct threat to the fractured psyche's negative narrative it formed about the "individual self" following the past traumatic life event(s) in it's limited way to cope and move on from the trauma.

The mind also does not believe the individual has earned the right to feel good about themselves now or to feel security or happiness.

After all, the individual is thought to have been indifferent and inept in the past to provide similar happiness, security to their mind when the individual failed to stop or prevent the early trauma from happening. So basically it is pay-back time and gambling is the means to exact the fractured mind's revenge.

That being said, the fractured mind also relies on challenging life events as an opportunity to push the individual self to the brink of despair because that is a time the individual self is more vulnerable and distracted to resist the self-destructive urges their mind presents as a solution to their current crisis or strife.

DIFFICULTIES / HARDSHIPS IN LIFE

The" individual self" is experiencing some personal, emotional or financial crisis, is feeling low, depressed, lonely, etc due to:

- Serious accident or injury

- Becoming a victim of personal / financial crime

- Being assaulted / exposure to abuse / constant bullying at work / home

- They or a loved one is diagnosed with a terminal Ilness

- Loss of a loved one

- Losing a job / Inability to find work

- Relationship challenges / break-up / divorce

- External emergency / crisis that jeopardizes one's home

(e.g., fire, flood, tornado, earthquake)

These types of dire life events can subject the individual to extreme negative emotional / mental stressors that their fractured psyche will look to exploit further as it sees this as an ideal opportunity to finally be able to push the "individual self" closer to the edge of despair, destruction and ruin just so its negative narrative it formed can be further justified and validated.

Also, whenever the problem gambler returns from a devastating gambling loss they are overcome with all sorts of negative emotions and self-deprecating thoughts. These negative and highly charged emotions of self-loathing, disgust, anxiety, fear, etc.. all satiate their fracture mind because it validates the negative view the mind formed about the individual self as well as leading the individual self to feel the pain and agony the fractured mind experienced when the individual failed to protect it in the past.

For the unsuspecting "individual self" who repeatedly falls for the deceptive ways with which addiction / high risk behavior urge(s) are presented by their fractured psyche as brimming with wonderful opportunities to change their life for the better - they soon find their life spiraling out of further control without realizing or understanding why they continue to allow this to happen.

Subsequently, most will find themselves sucked further and deeper into the dark abyss of despair as their addiction grows in frequency and intensity - until there is truly nothing left for them to lose except for the last and most precious commodity each person possesses - "THEIR LIFE".

It is at this moment - when all appears lost once the addict finds themselves hitting the ultimate rock bottom - that their fractured psyche steps up its game plan and presents suicide as the ideal solution that is brimming with even greater hope for a way out to a peaceful eternal existence.. These presented suidal thoughts are carried out in the same deceptive manner with which gambling urges were presented. The individual self is channeled to view taking their own life as a courageous and brave step brimming with the opportunity start over. Suicide is also not pitched as escaping life's turmoil and hardships rather reclaiming one's right to be free and happy and at peace.

Given the high incidence rate of suicides and suicide attempts around the world among gambling addicts (where many of their suicides may not even be captured appropriately by current statistics particularly among those battling a behavior addiction like compulsive gambling) - makes one wonder if it was not the fractured psyche's ultimate end goal right from the start - to lead the "individual self" to take their own life once everything and anything that offered them an anchor to live, gave them pleasure and a sense of value, needed to be eliminated first through the use of the alluring self-destructive urges that the mind presented so deceptively throughout the course of the addiction(s).

So perhaps, it is of value to start recognizing that the gambling addiction or other forms of high risk self-destructive compulsive behaviors are nothing more than the necessary vehicle / means that the individual's fractured subconscious mind needs and relies on to systematically eliminate all that which provide the individual a reason to live. And once all that the individual self holds dear and affords them with meaning to live for are gone - the final nudge to ending it all becomes more readily to execute.

The subconscious mind's motivation is to validate the negative narrative it had formed after the earlier life trauma as well as to punish the individual self for failing to protect it and not helping to heal it afterwards. By continuing to present opportunities for self-destruction the fractured psyche is basically navigating the addict to the edge from which they will take their final leap of faith of trusting their mind's last ditch effort to pitch death as the only way to finally achieve the peace and freedom they so desperately have yearned for. Through this last "fatal" decision and action to ending their life - their fractured psyche hopes to achieve its ultimate validation that it was correct all along about the individual self being weak and lacking any courage and holding no inclination for self-preservation, no self-worth nor strength to protect themselves or their mind from serious harms - even death.

To help individuals particularly those struggling with problem gambling prevent this tragic end from occurring, it is imperative for them to first acknowledge they have a problem and that their addiction is out of their control where they need to enter recovery without delay to get the needed support and insights including tools to end the "BLEED" their addiction is causing. In addition, what is also imperative is for those struggling with addiction to recognize that their addiction is a symptom of a much deeper underlying root cause that is using a high risk self-sabotaging behavior as a lure to seek their demise.

Recovery programs like the 12 steps program are superb at offering tools and support to help addicts abstain and better manage their urges so that their financial, emotional, social, "BLEED" will stop. The recovery program of choice will also afford all to reconnect socially with others for reasons mentioned earlier in this book.

By learning to abstain effectively and not give into future gambling urges they will be enabled to slowly reclaim their power back from their fractured psyche as it will dsicover that it is no longer successful to lure the individual self back into self-destructive behaviors patterns.

Once the fractured psyche takes notice of the "individual self" actions and that they are capable of safeguarding themselves against the harms that the gambling addiction presents - the fractured psyche will often test the individual self further. Where it will switch its game plan by presenting other new forms of self-destructive behaviors to get the individual self back to destroying all that remains dear in their life.

That is why it is imperative for the individual to not just learn how to avoid / resist their gambling urges but also to be alert and wise to other types of self-destructive urges that their fractured mind will want to present to them in hopes to validate its negative beliefs once again by luring the individual back to destroying themselves

By anticipating and recognizing the mental processes involved when it comes to behavior addiction and the recovery process will help prepare the individual better to deal and treat the root cause behind the addiction instead of just learning to abstain or learning to manage the symptoms of their addiction.

The problem gambler who enters a recovery program needs to commit fully to their recovery journey and learn to abstain from urges at all costs because their fractured mind is watching them and their actions closely to determine if it can ever trust the individual self again to do the right thing and protect both of them from risks and associated harms in the future. Only when the addict's fractured psyche comes to the realization by seeing the individual reclaiming control over their life with confidence and purpose by not engaging in self-destructive behaviors when old or new types of urges are being presented (by their subconscious mind) as a test - is when the actual recovery breakthrough happens.

It is at that point when the fractured psyche concedes and finally starts to accept that its earlier negative narrative it had formed about the individual self was incorrect and that it is time to allow the individual self to help it start healing by processing the past traumatic events properly and also to start trusting the individual self again. Once the individual self and their subconscious mind reestablish such trust is when the true healing has happened where together they become a formidable team that is better equipped to protect that which they both hold dear as well as embrace new opportunities in life that promote harmony, peace, a sense of self-worth and an appreciation for all good things that life has to offer.

To learn more about the Fractured Psyche Addiction Recovery Model construct and other addiction and harm reduction resources offered by Remedy Max please visit:
https://remedyblox.com/addiction-%26-recovery

ACTIVITY SECTION

What Hit Home?

Consider what has been read and take time to 'digest' it.

REVIEW

"Another masterfully written book by author Bernard Zeitler, where he guides the reader to view addiction and recovery through a new revolutionary lens. One where addiction is revealed as a chronic illness that requires a long term fluid and dynamic treatment approach to help the addict heal as well as become better equipped to deal and respond in a healthy way to various life events and personal circumstances that otherwise could become a trigger for relapse or create new avenues for onset of another addiction vice.

Through the use of carefully selected real life examples, the author draws on his personal experiences to illustrate the onset of addiction and its progressive nature with long term adverse effects on the individual. The author also explains that addiction is not an anomaly that is attributed to some moral defect or personal weakness of the individual battling addiction or struggling with self-destructive urges that create progressive social isolation, feelings of despair, fear and personal anguish. Similarly, the purpose and meaning of recovery is explored including its shortcomings if one attempts to merely measure recovery success by frequency of attendance or one's length of abstinence. Rather, working one's recovery needs to entail a fluid, pliable long term healing process that is all encompassing with a focus on treating the addiction's chronic nature. Especially since many in recovery still can and do relapse or end up acquiring another type of addiction after achieving long term abstinence from the original addiction that led them to seek rehabilitation in the first place.

Those who have struggled with urges and who find themselves relapsing will find this book of particular value as they will come to see their addiction(s) in a new light as well as discover an untapped internal strength, new found courage to release the past, gain self-forgiveness and embrace a brighter future that their addiction overshadowed and tried to destroy. Lastly, this book includes ample of activity pages after each chapter to help the reader journal and work through exercises that have been specifically designed for personal reflection and growth." - Remedy Max, M.A., President/CEO of RemedyBlox and founder of the Fractured Psyche Addiction Recovery Model.

Made in the USA
Columbia, SC
28 June 2023

19509663R00053